The Cat and the Tao

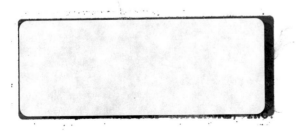

The Cat
and the Tao

KWONG KUEN SHAN

ATRIA BOOKS

New York London Toronto Sydney Singapore

ATRIA BOOKS

1230 Avenue of the Americas
New York, NY 10020

ISBN: 0-7434-5335-2

First Atria Books hardcover printing November 2002

10 9 8 7 6 5 4 3 2 1

ATRIA BOOKS is a trademark of Simon & Schuster, Inc.

For information regarding special discounts for bulk purchases,
please contact Simon & Schuster Special Sales at 1-800-456-6798
or business@simonandschuster.com

Printed in the U.S.A.

ACKNOWLEDGMENTS

The author would like to thank the following for their kind permission
to reproduce the paintings in this book:

Darley Anderson, Malcolm Johns, Ingrid Pieters, Zena Robson
and others who wish to stay anonymous.

Thanks also to the people who kindly allow her to paint their cats
and use the paintings in this book.

INTRODUCTION

I suffered from cat phobia. I never had a cat until six years ago. My first cat adopted me. Healey belonged to my ex-neighbour. They moved away taking all their cats with them. Healey returned four times to the land where he was born and brought up. The fourth time my husband and I felt we had to keep him on humanitarian grounds.

For a year he was kept outside and fed out in all weather. I could not bring myself to touch him, let alone allow him into the house. I knew the fear was irrational. I froze every time he was near me. Quietly and patiently he changed all that. I have had more cats since.

At the time I was developing a new painting project and something was missing in the plan. One day while gardening I saw Healey sunbathing between me and the stone buddha, our garden gnome. He curled around the buddha, looking relaxed and happy. I found the missing element.

What seemed to be a good idea at the time landed me on a very steep learning curve. I had no knowledge of cats. I had never painted them before. An amazing journey began. I started observing and studying cats; my own cats, Healey, Rocco and Joseph; other people's cats, stray cats. I was totally charmed by their elegance, agility, resilience, and above all their independence and mental toughness. I wanted to capture all these in the only way that I know, the Chinese way. It took me two years to produce enough sketches to work from, but now I have an ever expanding cat album. They are painted in Chinese styles with Chinese tools, materials, techniques and perspective. I have exhibited these paintings several times.

I painted the pictures in this book using both the meticulous and freestyle techniques. The meticulous method involves detailed drawing and refined elaboration, while the freestyle uses deceptively simple and economical brush strokes to capture the character and spirit of the subject. It is not concerned with detail.

My understanding of cats continues to develop and my affection for them to grow. I want to do more with these lovely creatures who share our lives. I want to share my appreciation of them with others, for them to see my vision of cats! I want to add an extra dimension to my cat album, and I have drawn on my knowledge of Chinese literature to achieve this.

I studied classical Chinese literature, history, and calligraphy as a child growing up in Hong Kong. This contact continues. While my husband reads English books, I read my collection of old and new Chinese books: Confucius's teaching, 300 Tang Poems, Dreams of the Red Chambers, Zen, Sun Tzu's Art of War and contemporary Chinese literature. So many of the wise say-

ings in these classic texts cry out to be linked with a painting, to illustrate
and be illustrated, to illuminate and inspire. I have had a wonderful time
seeking out the best match for each picture, and then translating them
into English.

Many books have been published on cats. I have tried to do a different
kind of cat book. My paintings of cats should depict them in action, at
rest, when they are aloof or tough, philosophical or just themselves,
though never humble! My hope was to combine feline character and
wisdom with appropriate oriental philosophy and teaching, to point out
the Way towards some answers to man's quest for respite from everyday
stress.

When I speak of the Tao, I do not mean Taoism as such, and I am not
talking about Taoism in this book. Tao is used here in the generic sense,
meaning the way to wisdom and inspiration. It means a direction for a
journey from beginning to end. It refers to the way we search for the
truth, the way we conduct ourselves. It means observing the law of
nature, living in harmony with other living things, and distinguishing
what is important to life from what is accessory.

The texts in this book are selected from ancient Chinese proverbs,
poems, and sayings of great teachers: Confucius, Lao Tse, Chong Tse and
Sun Tzu. Their teachings have played a major part in shaping Chinese

thought for centuries. They have handed down templates for life which can be used by anyone in any circumstances. The choice of quotes in this collection is based on their sympathetic resonance with the paintings, and personal taste. I translated them all from the original Chinese. Ancient Chinese literature is very condensed, very crisp, and a great deal is contained in a few words. There is no standard English version, and I have tried hard to preserve the vision, the truth and essence of the original text. I hope I have succeeded in sharing with you their meaning and wisdom.

I hope you will enjoy my book, and if it inspires you, so much the better!

KKS 2002

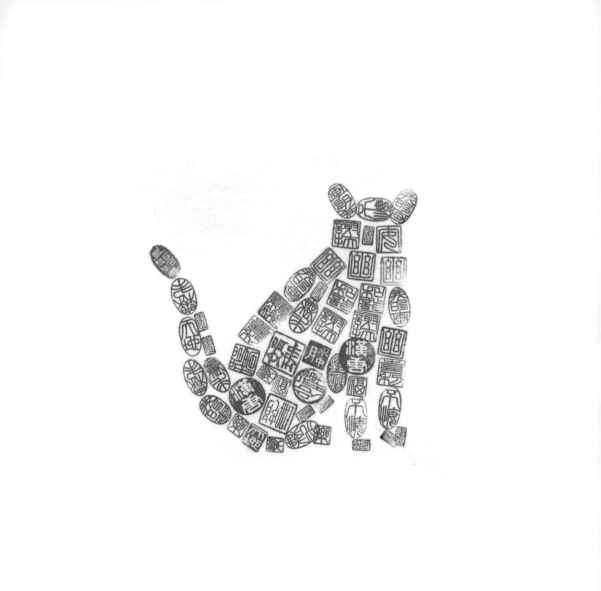

To know is to recognise what you understand
and what you do not understand.

CONFUCIUS

THE UNSPOKEN

Small seal: The Way | *Oval seal: Heaven and earth* | *Square seal: Kwong Kuen Shan*

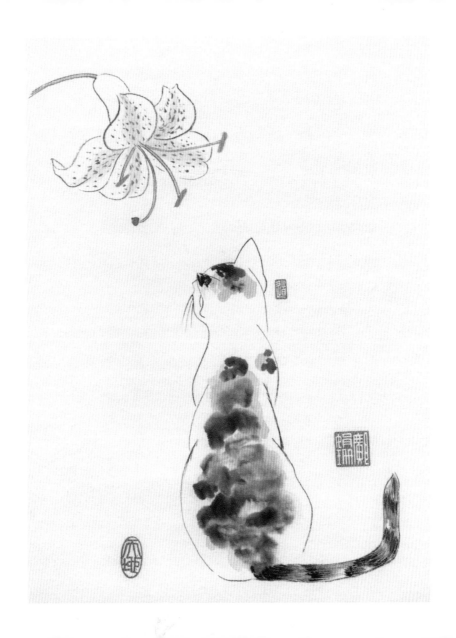

These days the world's events are strange:
They say this and they say that.
There is no point arguing.
I am better off dozing.

ANON

SPRING DREAMS

Chinese characters: on a nice day like today we should be singing and drinking wine.
Oval seal: I paint what I like | Rectangular seal: The Way
Round seal: Han and Tang Dynasties | Square seal: Kuen Shan

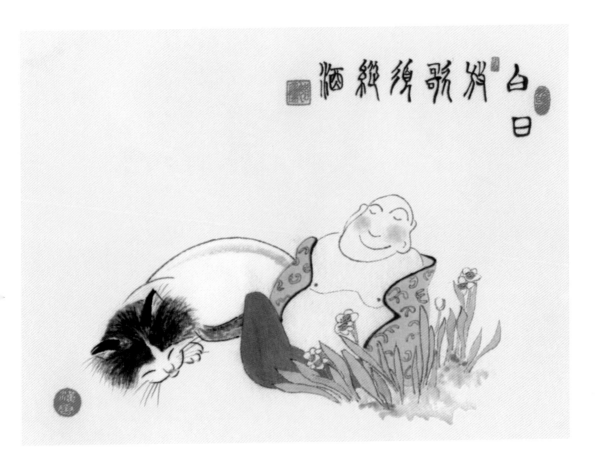

A man of great character and strength:
fire cannot burn him,
water cannot drown him,
the severest weather does not damage him,
wild beasts cannot rend him,
not because he is invincible,
but because he knows safety from danger,
he is calm and decisive even facing great risks,
he knows when to go forward, when to retreat,
nothing can harm such a man.

CHONG TSE

THE KUNG FU CAT

Rectangular seal:The Way | *Small square seal: Blessing* | *Square seal: Kuen Shan*

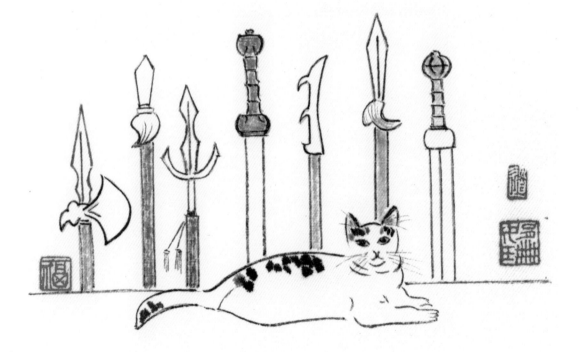

Do not exhaust a friend's kindness and loyalty
– this way friendship is sustained.

CHINESE PROVERB

MONTY AND MIZOO

Seal: Kwong Kuen Shan

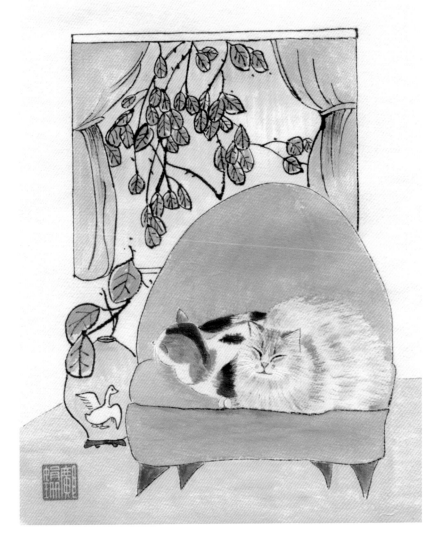

To find out what a person is like, there are seven ways:
Ask him a difficult question, observe his talent for analysis
Speak to provoke him, observe his attitude
Ask him how he goes about solving difficult problems,
    judge his intelligence
Let him deal with a difficult situation, observe his courage
Get him drunk, observe his nature
Tempt him with gold, observe his integrity
Give him instructions to complete a task, assess his
    trustworthiness.

THE ART OF WAR BY SUN TZU

SAFFRON

Square seal: Kwong Kuen Shan

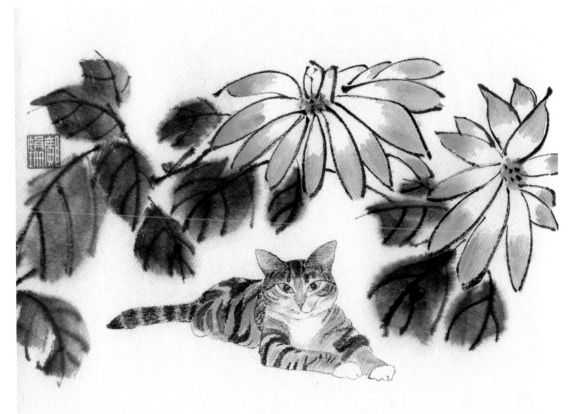

Seize the opportunity when it arises
Once missed, it may be lost forever.

FENG MENGLONG

JOSEPH

Round seal: Insight | *Oval seal: Heaven and earth*

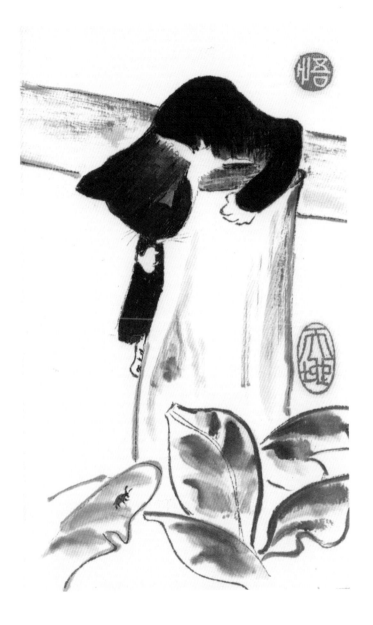

To know what is going on takes sense;
To know what to do about it takes wisdom.

CHINESE PROVERB

ON THE WINDOW

Round seal: Insight | *Rectangular seal: The Way*

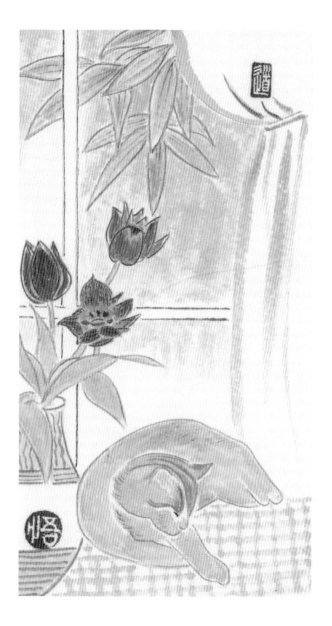

From day to day he knows what is lacking
From month to month he does not forget what
    he has learnt
This is a person who is truly inspired by learning.

CONFUCIUS

THE STUDIO

Small seal: The Way | *Square seal: Kwong Kuen Shan*

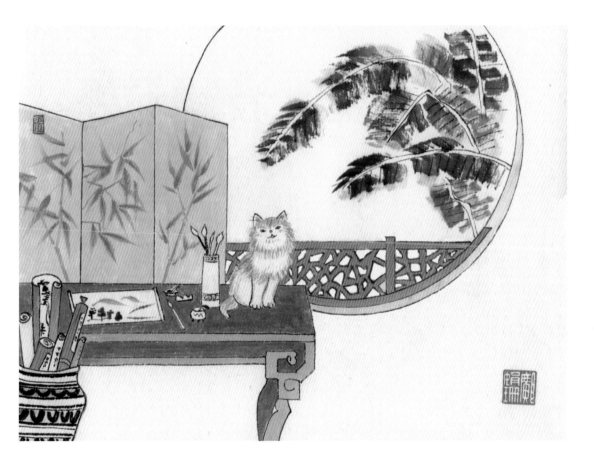

I do not value those who broadcast others' failings, subordinates who slander their superiors, those who are brave but lack manners, those who are decisive but lack consideration.

CONFUCIUS

A MAGNOLIA BRANCH

Chinese calligraphy: It's not me | *Oval seal: My painting* | *Rectangular seal: The Way*
Small square seal: Blessing | *Square seal: Kuen Shan*

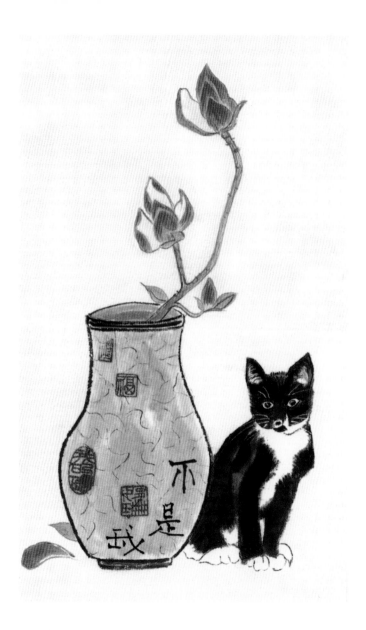

I do not bully the weak, nor do I fear the powerful.

ZUO QUINING

JOSEPH AND THE FISH

Small seal: The Way | *Oval seal: Heaven and earth*

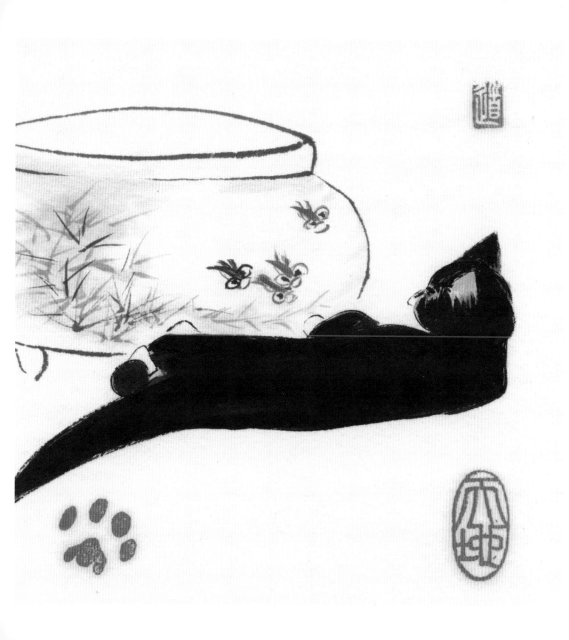

The ears and eyes are not made to think
and are easily affected by outside influences
The mind thinks, and if it thinks, it arrives at the truth.

CONFUCIUS

AUTUMN SERENADE

Square seal: Kwong Kuen Shan

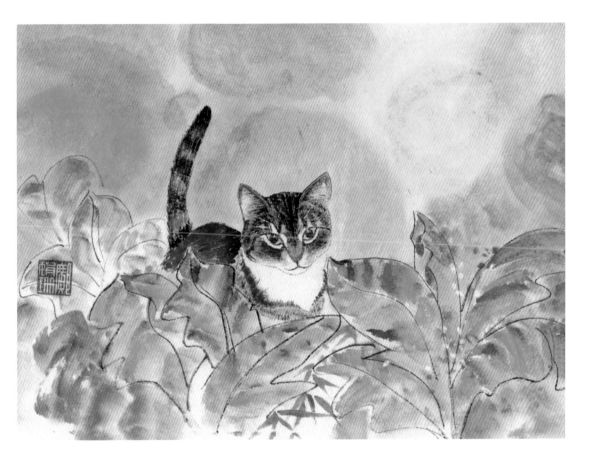

A great talker uses few words.

MENCIUS

BLUE EYES

Seal: Insight

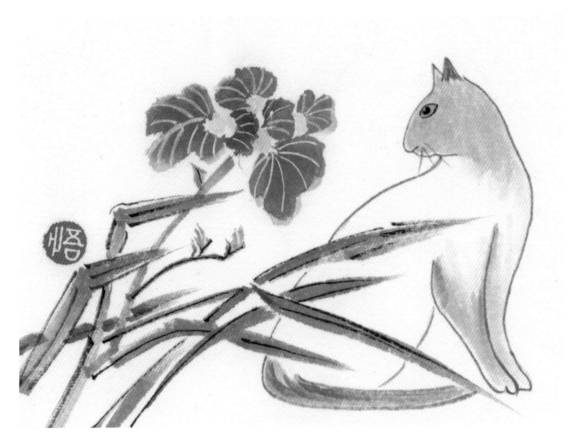

He who is over-courteous is tiring

He who is overcautious is fearful

He who is brave beyond reason is dangerous

He who is straightforward beyond consideration offends.

CONFUCIUS

HEALEY

Chinese characters: lost in low cloud | Round seal: Han and Tang Dynasties
Oval seal: My painting | Small square seal: Moon in water | Large square seal: Kuen Shan
Qing Dynasty pottery motif

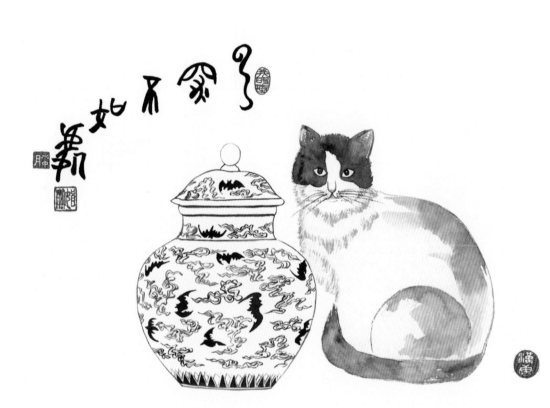

Do not take it to heart when you lose,
Do not show it on your face when you win.

GAO BOGONG

BIJOU

Seal: Kwong Kuen Shan

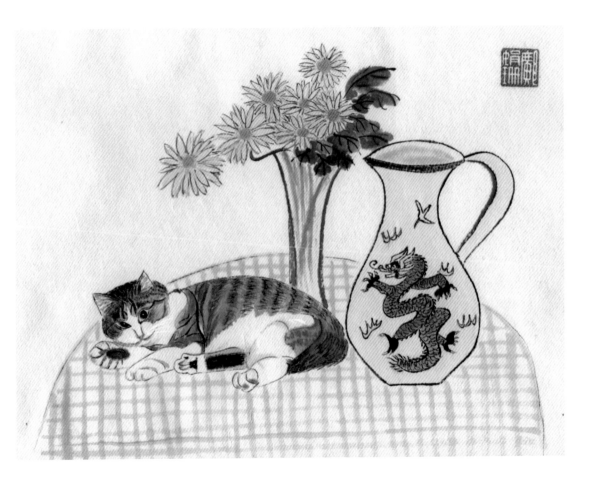

Three types of friendship are beneficial:
they are friendships with the honest, the
sincere and the well-informed.
Three types of friendships are damaging:
they are friendship with flatterers, with
hypocrites and with the argumentative.

CONFUCIUS

GOOD COMPANIONS

Chinese characters: good companions | *Oval seal: My painting*
Small round seal: Insight | *Large round seal: Predetermined encounter*
Square seal: Kuen Shan

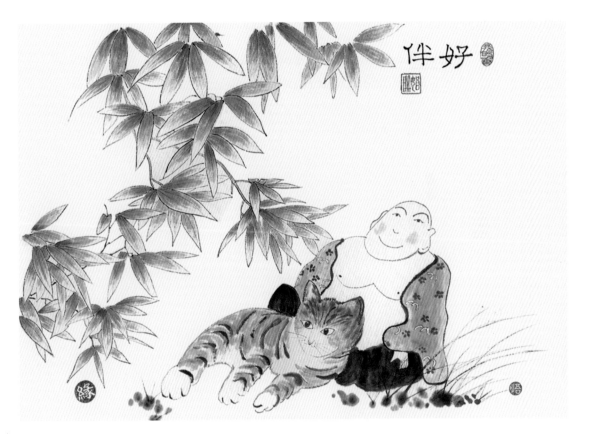

The roughest roads are not found across rivers and mountains, but in people's hearts.

BAI JUYI

WHEN HOME CALLS

Round seal: Insight | *Square seal: Kwong Kuen Shan*

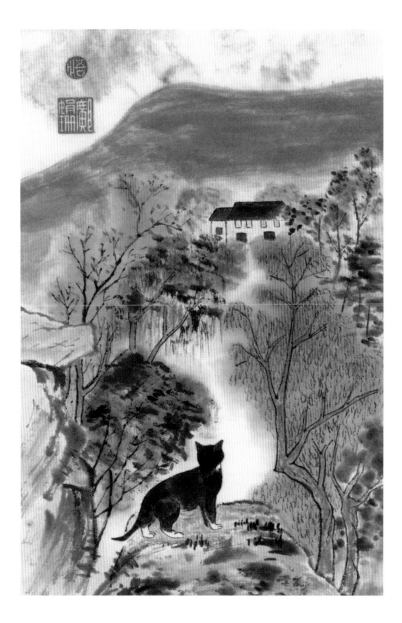

A wise man pays special attention to nine areas:

He sees with clarity; he hears distinctly;

He speaks sincerely; his countenance is gracious;

His manner is courteous; at work he strives for respect;

When in doubt he seeks information;

When angry he thinks of the negative consequences
    of his anger;

When he sees possible gain and profit he reflects on
    ethics and integrity.

CONFUCIUS

FACE TO FACE

Chinese characters: our true selves | *Small long seal: The Way* | *Small round seal: Insight*
Large round seal: Predetermined encounter | *Square seal: Kuen Shan*
Ming Dynasty pottery motif

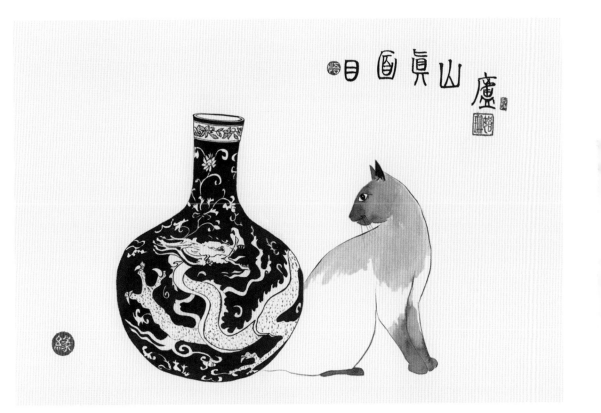

A friend who truly knows you is always with you.

CHINESE PROVERB

TWO BROTHERS

Chinese characters: brothers | *Oval seal: My painting* | *Square seal: Kwong Kuen Shan*

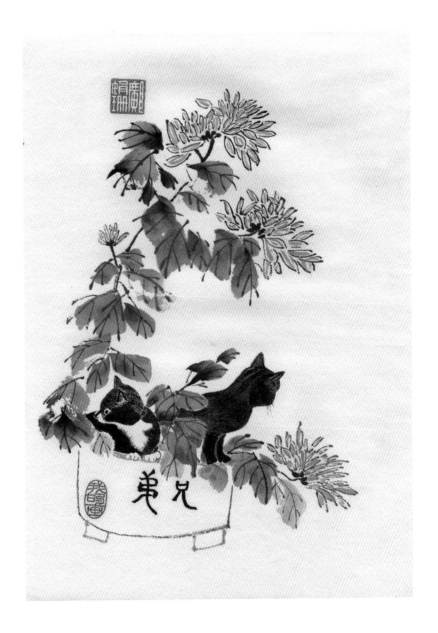

Only the very knowledgeable and the very ignorant do not shift their ground.

CONFUCIUS

THE BIRD TABLE

Rectangular seal: The Way | *Square seal: Kwong Kuen Shan*

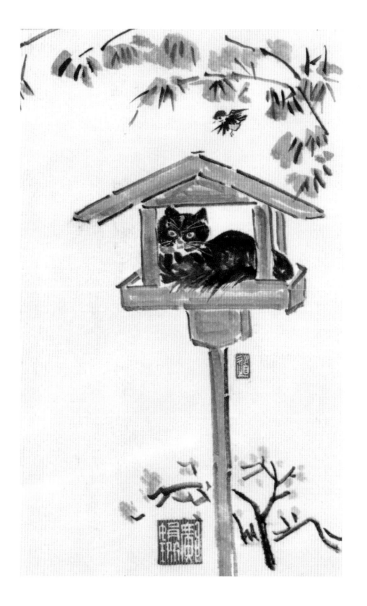

A wise man seldom fails because he anticipates problems.

FENG MENGLONG

HOMER

Seal: I have done it all, I need strive no more

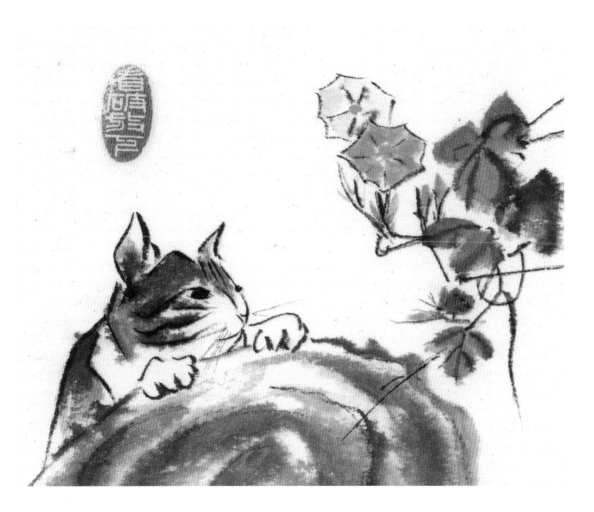

The usefulness of wisdom lies in the right application.
A wise man may fail because he considers too much,
while a fool may succeed by acting correctly only
once at the right moment.

FENG MENGLONG

CHING CHING

Chinese characters: I'm a charmer | *Square seal: Kuen Shan*

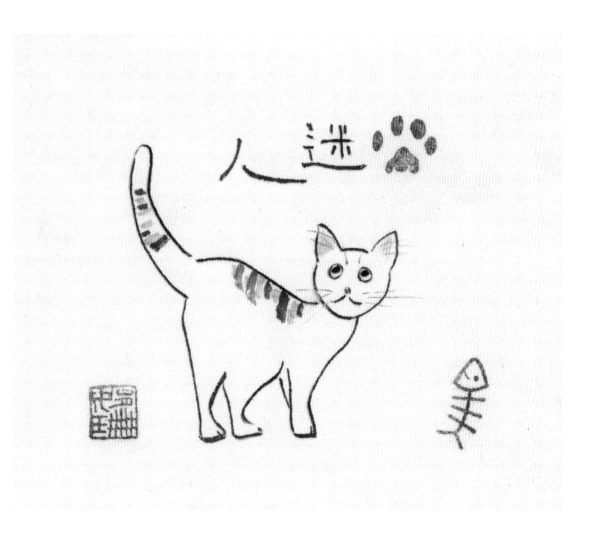

People rage, I do not.
Rage makes you ill, rage can kill,
rage wastes energy, rage sacrifices peace.

ANON

ZEN

Chinese characters: I've had a most wonderful day | *Seal: Heaven and earth*

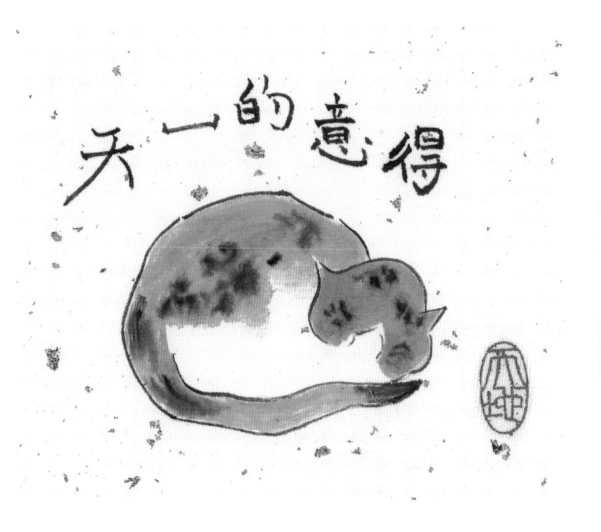

Those who do not attempt everything accomplish something.

MENCIUS

FIRST CATCH

Seal: Kwong Kuen Shan

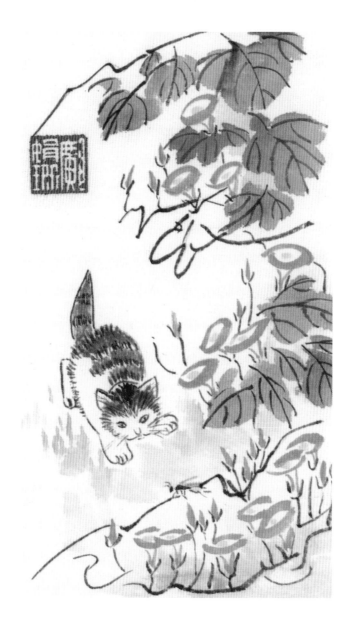

I do not value those who steal ideas and believe
themselves clever.
I do not value those who boast and believe
themselves courageous.
I do not value those who reveal the secrets of others
and believe themselves honest.

ZI GONG

THE DISCIPLE

Chinese characters: life's little stories | *Oval seal: My painting*
Small square: Moon in water | *Medium square: Meditation*
Large square seal: Kuen Shan

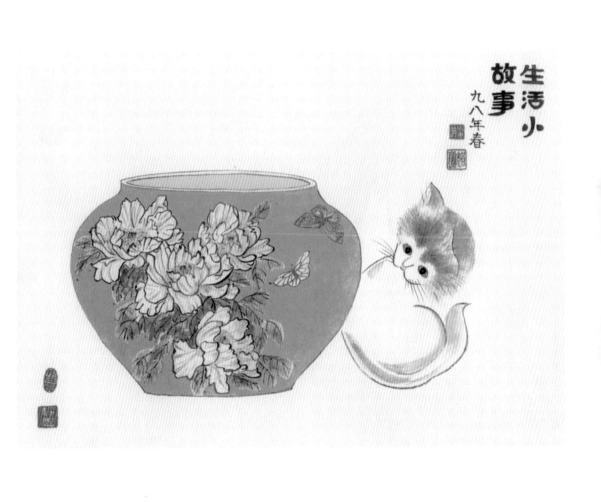

生活小
故事
九八年春

The less you know, the more confident you are.

CHINESE PROVERB

THE SNOWMAN

Seal: Insight

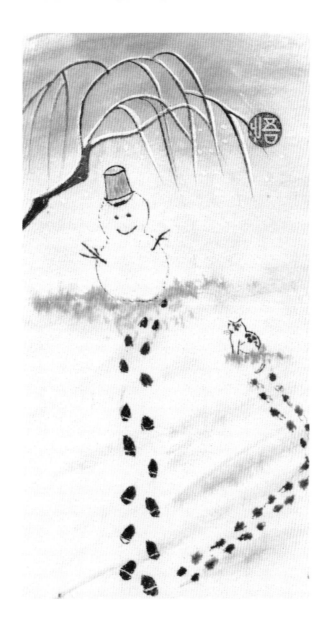

River dwellers know the way of the fish,
Mountain dwellers know the song of the birds;
River dwellers live off the river,
Mountain dwellers live off the mountain.

CHINESE PROVERB

BY THE RIVERBANK

Seal: Kwong Kuen Shan

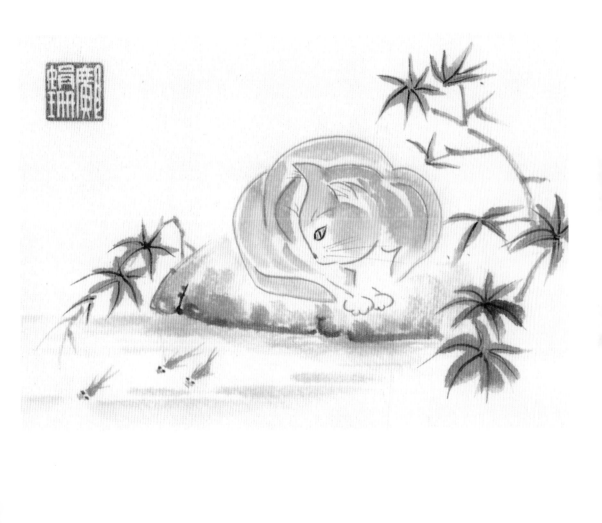

Prompt decision often succeeds,
Hesitation often fails.

LU XUOXUN

LOTUS

Seal: Kwong Kuen Shan

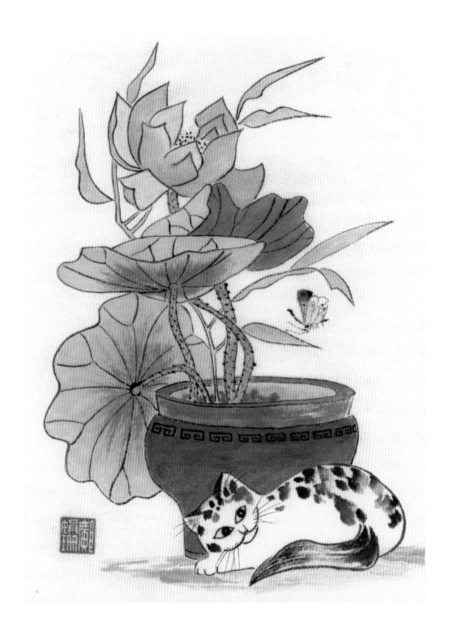

The virtuous man is never alone,
he has many like-minded friends.

CONFUCIUS

BUMPER HARVEST

Small seal: The Way | *Square seal: Kwong Kuen Shan*

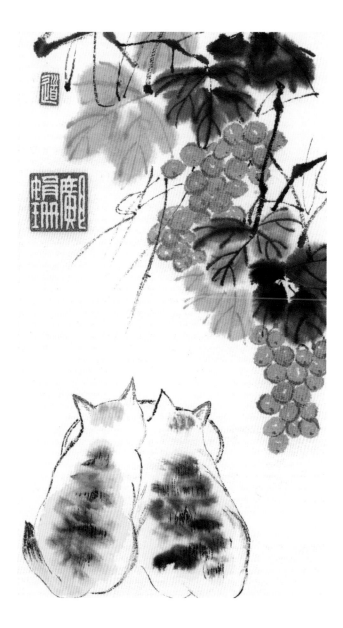

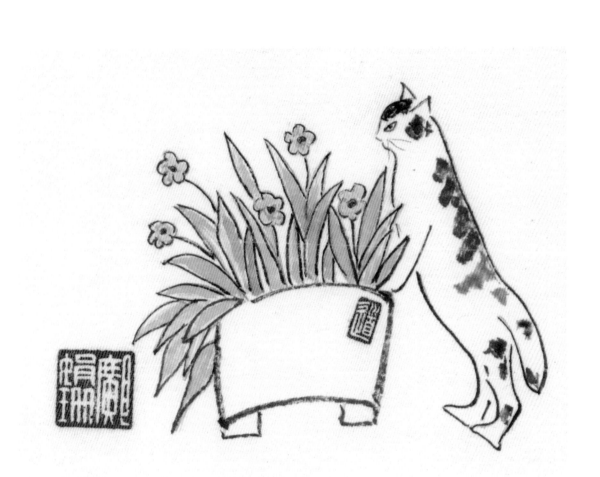

Three men bring trouble on themselves:
The ignorant man who follows his judgement,
The stubborn man who follows his will,
The contemporary man who wants to
   re-create the past indiscriminately.

CONFUCIUS

SCARECROW

Round seal: Insight | *Rectangular seal: The Way*

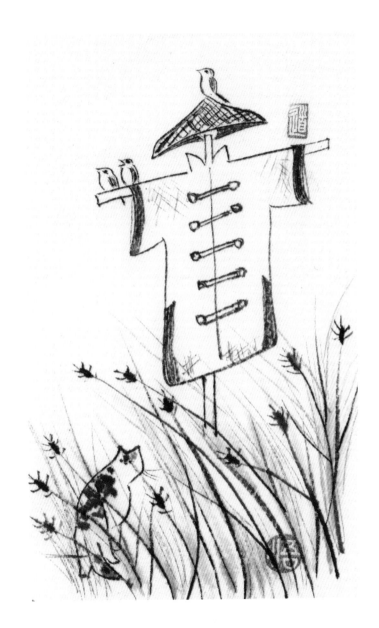

The advantage of being tiny:
Like a blade of grass looking up at a tree,
Like a stream looking out on the ocean,
Like a light in a village hut looking up
    at the stars in the sky;
Because being tiny,
I can see what is great.

ANON

GROWING UP

Small seal: The Way | *Square seal: Kwong Kuen Shan*

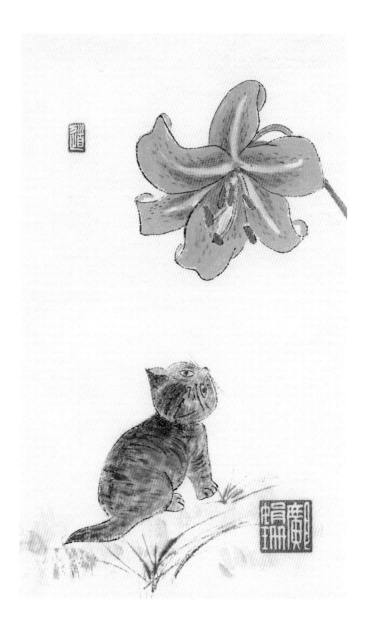

Ancient scholars studied for self-fulfillment;
Today's scholars study for fame.

CONFUCIUS

THE STUDY

Small seal: The Way | *Small square seal: Blessing* | *Square seal: Kwong Kuen Shan*

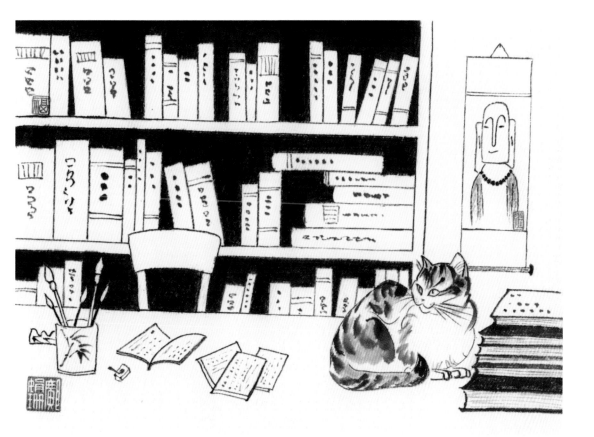

An intelligent person understands others,
A brilliant person understands himself.

CHINESE PROVERB

GIZMO

Seal: Insight

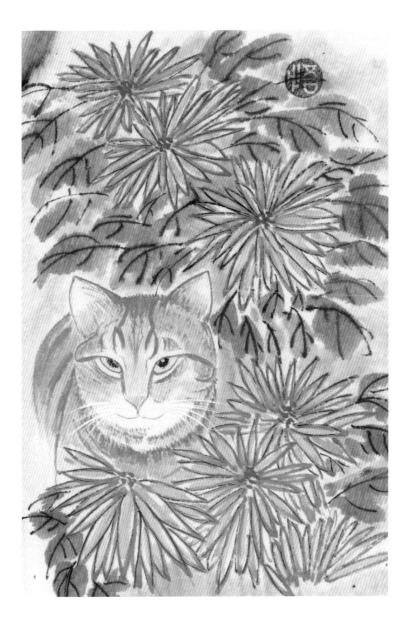

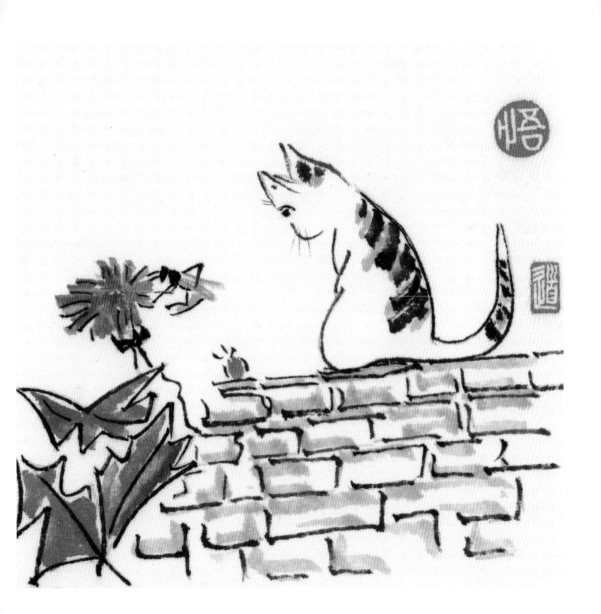

A broad-minded person finds even a
small space accommodating.

CHINESE PROVERB

THE COURTYARD

Chinese characters: I find my own happiness
Round seal: Insight | Rectangular seal: The Way | Square seal: Kwong Kuen Shan

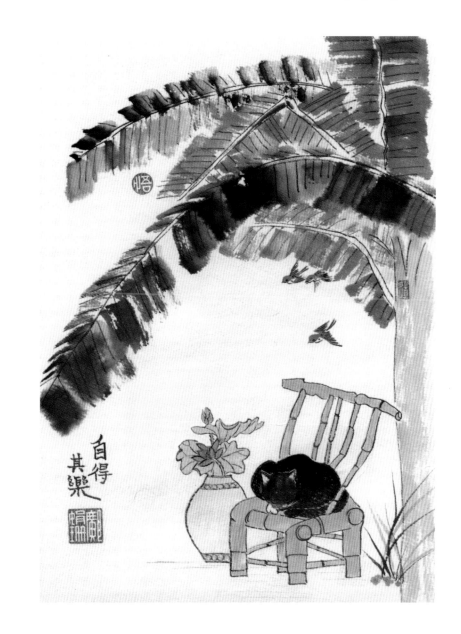

When I walk with two companions both would be my teachers:
I would choose the good traits and follow them, and would try
to correct in myself the faults I see in them.

CONFUCIUS

THREE FRIENDS

Round seal: Zen | *Oval seal:* Heaven and earth | *Square seal:* Kwong Kuen Shan

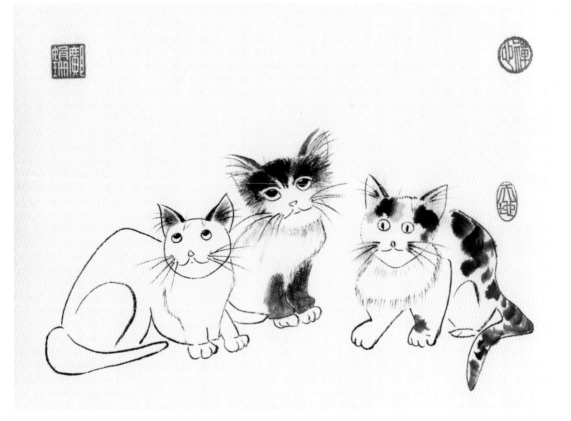

To be self-sufficient is to be happy,
To have no demands is to have no worry.

ANON

DO NOT DISTURB

Chinese characters: the joy of leisure | *Oval seal: Follow fate* | *Small round seal: Insight*
Large round seal: Han and Tang Dynasties | *Square seal: Kuen Shan*
Ming Dynasty pottery motif

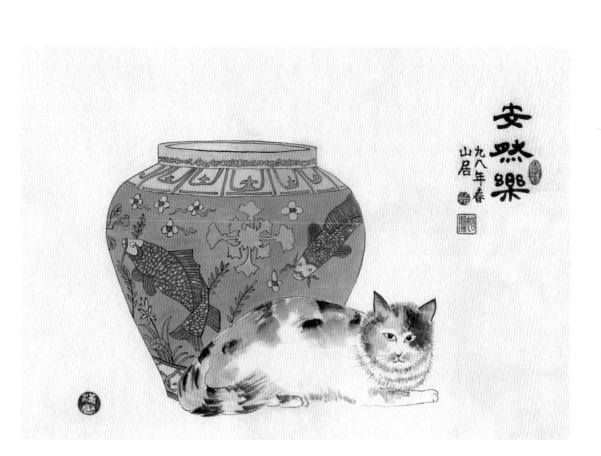

I beg you do not love your golden dress,
Rather value your youth.
Collect sweet blossoms while you can,
Do not wait till the branches are bare.

CHINESE POEM

BLACK VELVET

Small seal: The Way | *Square seal: Kwong Kuen Shan*

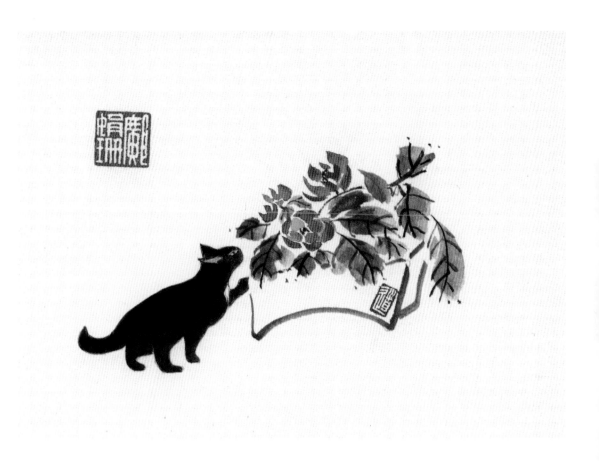

The wise man exercises his vigilance
where no one can see him – in his heart.

CONFUCIUS

AH MING

Small seal: The Way | *Square seal: Kwong Kuen Shan*

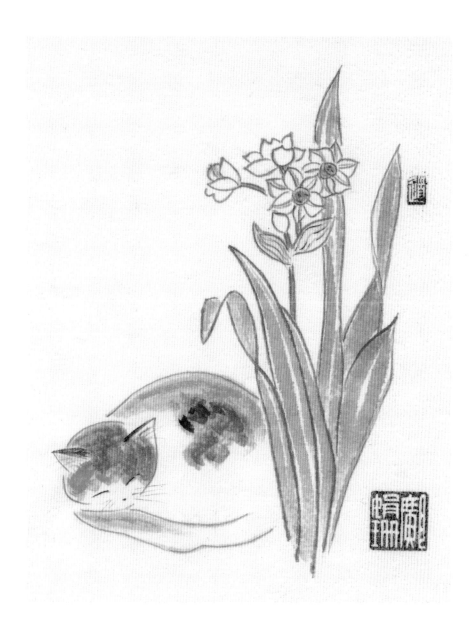

To judge a man, compare his words with his deeds.

LIU XIANG

BENSON

Round seal: Insight | *Oval seal: My painting* | *Square seal: Kwong Kuen Shan*

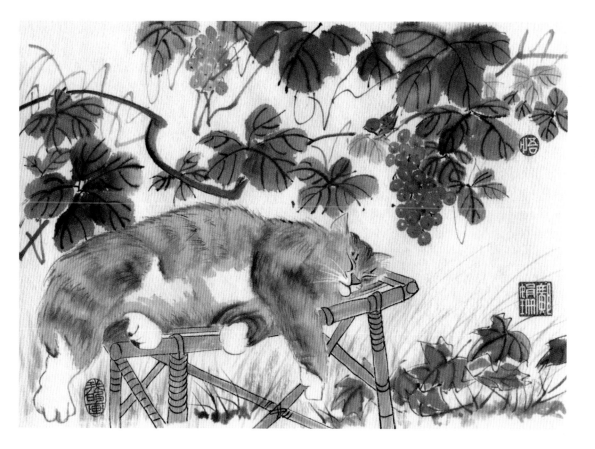

A COLLECTION OF SEALS

Reading from left to right and then top to bottom, the seals translate as follows:

1. Kuen Shan
2. Meditation
3. Kwong Kuen Shan
4. Heaven and earth
5. There is a light, next to my bed.
   Is it frost, white on the ground?
   I look up, it is the moon.
   I lie back, and think of home.
   TANG POEM BY LI PO
6. My painting
7. Predetermined encounter
8. Phoenix
9. Heart of Zen

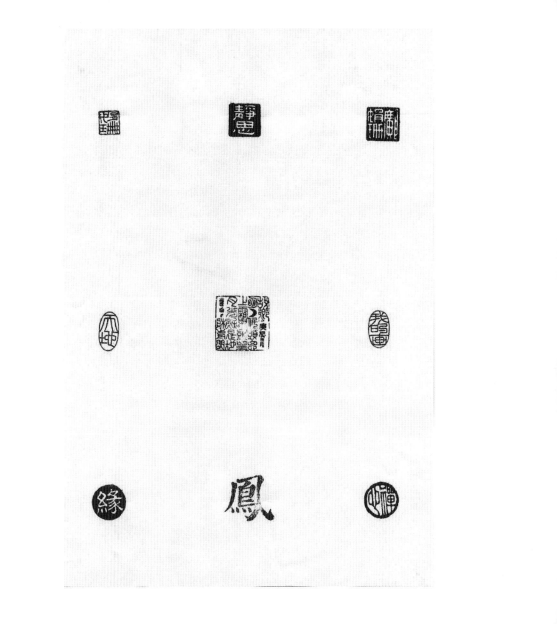

A COLLECTION OF SEALS

Reading from left to right and then top to bottom, the seals translate as follows:

1. I have done it all, I need to strive no more
2. Insight
3. Follow fate
4. The Way
5. Han dynasty subject: Kwong Kuen Shan
6. Blessing
7. Kuen Shan
8. Moon in water
9. Han and Tang Dynasties

EXPLANATORY NOTES ON SEALS

Seals you often see on Chinese paintings are Chinese characters carved from jade, ivory, soapstone or wood. They are pressed into cinnabar paste and then pressed in a suitable position on the painting to reproduce the characters. There are two main types of seals. One is the name seal which bears the name of the painter. The other is the 'mood' or 'leisure' seal which bears characters to reflect the mood, inspiration or philosophy of the painter.

KKS 2002

ABOUT THE AUTHOR

KWONG KUEN SHAN grew up in Hong Kong, where she studied classical Chinese and Chinese calligraphy. She later studied Chinese brush paintings and has been painting, exhibiting, and teaching her art for several years. She lives with her husband in Abergavenny, England.